IF YOU GIVE a MAN
≈ a PARODY ≈

Introduction

Jerry Seinfeld said that boys spend the first 10 years of their life trying to think of ways to get candy. Adolescent boys and men, according to reports, think about sex every few minutes.

There — now you have the life cycle of that gender.

Except for one more consistent through line that spans all those years – an abiding interest throughout life – in addition to candy and sex. **CARS**.

Now, that preoccupation is specifically about **TESLAs**.

We thought it deserved its own book.

PS – and now you know why they can't find the leftovers in the fridge, hidden in the front on the second shelf.

Text Copyright © 2021 by Renee Burns Lonner. All rights reserved.
Illustrations Copyright © 2021 by Christine Mallouf. All rights reserved.

ACKNOWLEDGEMENTS

Much gratitude for the love and support of my husband, son, daughter-in-law and two amazing grandsons – and for their endless supply of humorous material. They are just naturally funny, though most of the time that is not their intent.

To the rest of my family and friends who were supportive, offered suggestions and answered the question of whether this project was "creative or insane" correctly, I am most appreciative.

And as for the TESLA in our driveway, you're kinda cool looking. But I still think – not to be insulting – that a car is transportation, and its goal is to get you from point A to point B with no drama. So NOT how the other gender thinks.

IF YOU GIVE a MAN a TESLA
≈ a PARODY ≈

by Renee Burns Lonner

Illustrations by Christine Mallouf

If you give a man a TESLA, he will talk about it morning, noon and night – and we mean all the f***ing time.

Soon that means that . . .

he'll end up only talking to boys.

There are **three** kinds of boys – those who have one, those who want one and those who have ordered one and are waiting impatiently, counting days, like before their birthday or Chanukah or Christmas.

At social events, the boys will be in one group and the girls in another – just like middle school.

about "the range" as though it were
a jet and "ludicrous mode"
(yes, it is really a thing)
as if he were Dale Earnhardt.

He'll wax poetic about how much nicer this GPS lady is than the one in his last car.

Instead of snarling "Route Recalculation" to emphasize his mistake, she sweetly indicates the next correct turn.

This state of awe will make him think that his TESLA reads his mind, anticipates his needs and prevents him from getting into trouble, at least behind the wheel.

(If only he spent 1% of that time trying to figure out how the other gender worked, what a world this would be!)

He will be so captivated that he will read the entire 200-300-page manual

≈ and be tempted to print it out ≈

It might be the only book he has read in the last two years.

In fact, the last time he read any set of directions was to access Hulu.

That was one paragraph and he bitched about it for a week.

He'll be so delighted with his new knowledge that he'll want to impress other boys, so he'll start or join a poker group.

Then he'll listen to them talk about and compare their TESLAs' range and size and native intelligence.

On those driving trips, he will want to bet anyone in the car how far the TESLA can go on a single charge.

If his companion is a partner, should he bet money (no fun) or chores no one likes (minimal fun) or outrageous favors for which he gets a coupon book?

≈ okay, now we're talking ≈

On the way to those houses, **he'll be smug** as he passes dozens of gas stations and

he will wave in the most respectful way.

After he waves he'll still be smiling, so proud that he is reducing his carbon footprint on the planet and almost single-handedly halting climate change.

When others in the car **roll their eyes**, he'll terrify them by putting it on autopilot and pretending – for a moment – to take a nap.

Once back home he'll look for excuses just to drive around,
so he'll volunteer to take the kids to soccer practice and pick up dry cleaning.

Then he'll complain that his TESLA isn't big enough for all those kids, has a teeny-tiny "coat hook" that's no good for dry cleaning and the trunk is smaller than in his old car.

EPILOGUE

And now that his son thinks about it, **he** needs a new and smaller, remote-controlled TESLA to play along with his YouTube friends (who look like bigger kids but may be grown-ups).

But then that's the subject of a whole new book.

THE END

About

Renee Burns Lonner, author, is a management consultant for major corporations and a licensed psychotherapist based in Los Angeles, California. She has always loved writing and prior to this project, her work has been serious, appearing in professional publications, newspapers and a textbook. The pandemic and all its craziness provided the need for therapy of the literary kind, and the opportunity to observe a most humorous intersection of gender and culture presented itself. This book is the result.

reneelonner.com

Christine Mallouf, illustrator, is truly an artist's artist. Using her many talents across various mediums, she has worked in the advertising, fashion, photography and book illustration industries. Also, several animation studios in Los Angeles, including The Walt Disney Studios and Warner Brothers Animation, have benefited from her talents. Christine is currently the Director of Los Angeles Unified School District's Conservatory of Fine Arts for Gifted and Talented Students.

cmalloufla.blogspot.com

Made in the USA
Columbia, SC
21 July 2022